A Shelton Story

A SHELTON STORY

Memories of a Secrest Series of Events

by

Lillian Britt Shelton

with

Ken Keuffel

ISBN 978-1618460653

Cover image courtesy of Hayes Henderson

Produced and distributed by:

Library Partners Press
ZSR Library
Wake Forest University
1834 Wake Forest Road
Winston-Salem, North Carolina 27106

www.librarypartnerspress.org

Manufactured in the United States of America

With

everlasting appreciation

for

Wake Forest University

which encourages excellence
in all endeavors and supports its

staff and faculty

in so doing.

TABLE OF CONTENTS

Preface

LIFE CAN BE A SYMPHONY or a cacophony of sounds. In *A Shelton Story* we find harmony as the life of Lillian Shelton blends with the Secrest Artists Series. The process, like most good concerts, is developmental. In this volume, we discover how Lillian and the Secrest converged, merged, and surged into something more than anyone may have expected. The background of each is examined extensively. The intertwining of the two would never have been predicted in the early life of each. Yet, the unforeseen outcome is fascinating and intriguing to watch. The results are a progression that lifts them up and moves them forward into a place of respect and reverence in the hearts and minds of those at Wake Forest University and Winston-Salem, North Carolina, during the early part of the 21st century.

Rather than a humdrum series of disjointed segments that dance around chaotically, this book is a carefully constructed narrative. It flows in a graceful, informative, and unforgettable way. It shows the co-mingling of different experiences fluidly coming together for the enrichment of a community. It takes us behind the scene of flawless performances to see how they were constructed. Here we find the backstory of an ingenious and hardworking woman who made an outstanding artists series better yet. Lillian, on a shoestring budget, made a shoe. This history unfolds in insightful, delightful, and profound ways. It is worth an investment of time. Lillian and the Secrest created lasting memories. Those magical moments come alive again in *A Shelton Story*.

Samuel T. Gladding, Ph.D.
Professor of Counseling, Wake Forest University

Introduction

As DIRECTOR OF THE Secrest Artists Series at Wake Forest University from 1998 to 2013, I planned everything from programming each season to ensuring that all operations went smoothly behind the scenes. I am proud of what my many volunteer supporters and I accomplished during my tenure. Among other things, we:

- Enhanced students' appreciation of the performing arts by introducing them to some of the best musicians, dancers and actors;

- Demonstrated that forming alliances with the right people can accomplish lots of positive and significant things, from putting more novice patrons in seats to making a Secrest event the center of a mini-festival of lectures, seminars and exhibitions across several disciplines;

- Came up with effective ways to market the series, often drawing on the input of student interns, each of whom devised his or her own yearly plan for marketing the series to Wake Forest's student body;

- Gave interns their first real-world taste of arts administration; and

- Mattered in the larger scheme of things because programming decisions made in consultation with faculty advisors either affirmed the greatness of established talents or helped promising ones enhance their reputations.

In this memoir, I show how all this was done, devoting a different section to each of my main responsibilities as series director. On occasion, I also draw on my memories of the work I did for the Secrest Artists Series and for other employers before I became the Secrest director.

A Shelton Story has three aims. The first is to leave behind some helpful insights for current and future impresarios, both at Wake Forest and at other schools with similar series. The second is to enhance the collective appreciation of the challenges involved in making the Secrest Artists Series happen year after year. And the third is to share an entertaining anecdote or two.

A little Secrest 101: The Secrest Artists Series is named for Marion Secrest (1906-2013), a performing arts patron from Winston-Salem. In 1987, she endowed the series in honor of Willis Secrest, her late husband. However, money for the Secrest endowment was a planned gift that would not become available until after Marion's death; the series did not benefit from it until two months after I left Wake Forest. This meant that during my directorship, we operated on a bare-bones budget.

Despite these challenges – and much to the astonishment of my colleagues at other university presenters – we could and did hire the highest calibre of artists. That's because roughly half of Secrest's budget was dedicated to artist fees and there was only one paid staff: me. Ushers and box office personnel consisted of in-house volunteers.

First Things First

Thank You, Jay Lawson!

ANY ARTIST NEEDS FIRST-CLASS LIGHTING, staging, and sound engineering to give a first-class performance. Thus, the success of any performing arts series is dependent on the quality of its technical expertise.

Enter Jay Lawson, the technical director of Brendle Recital Hall and Wait Chapel, the two principal Secrest venues on campus.

Lawson and his "Jay's Crew" of undergraduate assistants faced numerous challenges. These ranged from presenting a 98-piece orchestra on Wait's stage, which was not built for performances by any large ensemble, to presenting a dance company on Brendle's stage, which had no backstage crossover, side lighting, wing space or dressing rooms. Despite all this, Jay and his assistants were always up to speed, no doubt inspired by Lawson's three rules of working: "with a sense of humor, without complaint, and quite hard."

After a few technical bumps emerged during the first few years of my directorship, Lawson and I agreed that, before signing a contract with a Secrest artist, I would require a tech rider in advance and he would review it. Although I had to pass on a few attractive artists and events, it was a good decision.

That left a continuing and challenging dilemma of choosing where to stage a presentation, namely Wait (seating 2,250) or Brendle (seating 560). Do we pack Brendle and potentially turn people away? Or do we put 1,000 patrons in cavernous Wait Chapel and make it appear as if no one attended?

Welcome to but one of my many decisions as the series' director!

Part I

My Road to Wake Forest University

A Military Brat Sees the World, Falls for the Arts

MY FULL NAME IS Lillian Britt Phillips Shelton, and I was born in Reno, Nevada. My father, Sidney Price Phillips, enjoyed a distinguished career in the military, piloting C46s and C47s during World War II and, later, specializing in electronics. All told, he served in the military for 23 years, most of them in the Air Force, which became a separate military branch in 1947. After retiring from the Air Force with the rank of lieutenant colonel, he worked for General Electric on the Apollo Project, contributing to the team that designed the lunar landing module.

I never spent much time in any one place during my childhood. That's because I lived the life of an itinerant military brat, moving where the Air Force moved my father. I lived on both United States coasts, the United Kingdom and Asia, joined by my mother, Lillian Caroline Bell Phillips, a Southern belle from southern Georgia, and my brother, Sidney Norris Phillips, who died of liver cancer in 2001.

Along the way, I developed an interest in the arts. I acted in plays, studied ballet and took piano and harp lessons. The arts gave me not only the creative outlet I craved but also a sense of community I could count on each time that our family moved to a new home. Along the way, I took in some memorable presentations: The first live theater performance I remember seeing was a Covent Garden production of *Aida* – which featured live elephants on stage. Our family lived in London from 1957 to 1961.

Eventually, my interest in the arts would become strong enough to influence my decision to pursue employment with what was then called the Artists Series at Wake Forest University. However, my path to arts administration was circuitous. Before Wake Forest appeared on my radar, I would move around a good bit, hold positions in several other fields, get married, and give birth to two children.

At one point, I even entertained notions of making it as an actress, having acted well in several school productions at St. Andrews Presbyterian College, which I attended in the 1960s. I earned a bachelor's degree in fine arts from St. Andrews, with an emphasis in theatre, graduating in 1966.

(The school, a liberal arts college in Laurinburg, North Carolina, was renamed St. Andrews University in 2011.)

Shortly after my college days ended, I moved into an attractive apartment in the Central Park West section of Manhattan. My three roommates were all women. Two were trying to make it in acting, one as a singer. After observing my roommates' struggles to find work over a three-week period, I sensed that I likely wasn't talented enough to pursue a career in show business, and, in any event, concluded that my roommates' life of hustling was not for me. I abandoned plans to audition for parts in shows.

Instead, I focused solely on my day job at the National Council of Churches (NCC), an ecumenical organization that worked for several causes, including justice, peace, and racial equality. My position there was Executive Secretary to the late Rev. Dean Kelley, Director of Religious Liberty in the Department of Social Justice. It was an interesting time to work at the NCC: Representatives from the Delta Ministry, a prominent civil rights group in Mississippi, along with civil rights leaders Andrew Young and the Rev. Jesse Jackson were among our visitors. Students at Columbia University and their allies marched near our offices to protest the Vietnam War.

I count Kelley among my most inspiring supervisors. In the 1970s, he authored two books that remain required reading for students of religion and politics: *Why Conservative Churches are Growing: A Study in Sociology of Religion* and *Why Churches Should Not Pay Taxes.*

During my tenure at the NCC, Kelley wrote that organization's "Statement on Conscientious Objection." I typed up the statement, a landmark document at the time, and made hundreds of copies of it. Unfortunately, a critical typo surfaced in the document I had typed. Kelley had to scramble to have it corrected just before it was presented to a meeting of NCC's General Assembly, which voted to adopt it at a meeting in Miami. This folly taught me a lesson that I would apply to my directorship of the series: Announcements, concert programs and other documents must be error-free.

After 18 months of secretarial work at the NCC, I noticed that my male college-graduate friends were making more money than I was and assuming managerial positions. I thought to myself: *What is wrong with this picture?* I started looking around for a job with more weight and scope for my imagination.

I Head to Newport, Get Married to a Sailor

A sympathetic woman in personnel at the NCC told me about a position with the Armed Services YMCA that had three memorable requirements: You had to be at least 24 years old, a college graduate and a Christian. I applied and was hired as Associate Program Director of the Armed Services YMCA in Newport, Rhode Island. The culture of my employer was very much reminiscent of the 1940s and '50s – and, really, much like the USO. I planned recreational activities and recruited volunteers to work with off-duty servicemen from the Newport Navy Base.

During my YMCA tenure, the Newport Navy Base was the headquarters for the Atlantic Destroyer Fleet. It was swarming with sailors, and, in time, I met and married one of the most handsome: Tom Shelton. Shortly after I had worked for six enjoyable years at the Armed Services YMCA, the Destroyer Fleet was moved from Newport and the YMCA was scaled back. I needed to find another job.

In 1974, I secured employment at the Adult Correctional Institute in Rhode Island working as a recreation director for the women and the teenage girls in the institute's detention center. In 1975, my husband's commitment to the Navy was concluded. He had served six years, two as a Reservist. He never saw duty in Vietnam. He served as a Gunner's mate and ASROC ("Anti-Submarine Rocket") technician, finishing as a Second-Class Petty Officer.

After Tom's stint in the Navy ended, he finished work toward his undergraduate degree at Barrington College, a now-defunct liberal arts Christian college in Barrington, Rhode Island. A little bit more about Tom's background:

He is a native of Winston-Salem, where, in the 1950s, his father took him to the groundbreaking ceremony for Wake Forest College, later renamed Wake Forest University. (The school, which moved to Winston-Salem in 1956, is named for its original location near Raleigh.) During the ceremony, President Harry Truman shoveled the ceremonial soil.

Tom's life goal was to become a minister in the Moravian Church, a fixture of his hometown's religious culture since the 18th century. So, after he graduated from Barrington College, we moved to Bethlehem, Pennsylvania., so that Tom could begin studies at Moravian Theological Seminary. In time, I found a position as Director of the Area Agency on Aging, a Northampton County agency in Bath, a small town near Bethlehem. The job entailed planning recreation and education programs and supervising meal preparations for Bath's elderly.

In 1978, Tom completed his seminary studies and was ordained. We moved to Clemmons, North Carolina, because of Tom's first minister position: Associate Pastor at Clemmons Moravian Church. In 1980, he accepted the call to become the Pastor at Rolling Hills Moravian Church in Longwood, Florida, which is very near Orlando. During that time, I occasionally worked as a saleswoman for a plant tissue culture firm that sold tissue cultures to the plant industry in Apopka. I also served as a substitute teacher at Lake Highland Preparatory School in Orlando.

Our Move to Winston-Salem Leads to My Job at Wake Forest University

In the summer of 1984, Tom was called to Friedberg Moravian Church in Winston-Salem, where he would serve as Senior Pastor for 29 years. By this time, our two children – daughter, Lillian Sidney Shelton Youngs, and son, Thomas Christian Shelton, both born in the 1970s – were in elementary school. I realized that I was growing restless as a full-time mother, having not worked consistently for seven years. I was ready to go back to work. In 1985, I started looking for a substantive part-time job.

In time, I came to focus my job search on Wake Forest University, figuring, rightly, that any position there would be interesting and that I would surely be working with smart people. Lacey Burcham, my contact in Wake Forest's personnel department, told me about an opening with the university's Artists Series (it had yet to be named for Marion Secrest): Dr. George Trautwein, the series' director at the time (and also an Associate Professor of Music and the conductor of Wake Forest's orchestra), was looking for a secretary, a new part-time position.

Initially, I wasn't all that enthusiastic. Such employment would be a step backward for somebody who'd once worked in management. Burcham knew that. I remember her telling me, "You're overqualified and you'll be underpaid." She said that she felt that the job would be a good fit for me because of my background in fine arts, not even mentioning my previous professional experience.

I swallowed my pride and applied. Trautwein interviewed me and I was hired.

My first series title was secretary. After a couple of years on the job, though, Trautwein changed my title to "coordinator" at my request. This better reflected my actual responsibilities and how I was performing them. I would be the series' coordinator for 11 years. In this capacity, my many duties included taking care of most pre-performance preparations; managing the front-of-house ushers and box office during performances; and overseeing the care and maintenance of artists. I watched and listened how Trautwein made artistic decisions and negotiated through contracts with artists' management agencies.

Part II

The Promotion

LOOKING BACK, I MUST HAVE SENSED that this job with the series could make me the kind of big fish in a small pond who could eventually take on leadership responsibilities and morph into a manager. That's exactly how my first 13 years at the series played out. I not only re-emerged as a manager but also became the first non-faculty director of a significant enterprise.

Dr. Samuel T. Gladding is Professor of Counseling in the Department of Counseling at Wake Forest University. In 1998, the year that Trautwein retired, Gladding began serving the university as an associate provost in charge of eight academic-support offices, one of these being the Secrest Artists Series.

Gladding appointed me the series' director immediately after Trautwein tendered his resignation. In an interview for this memoir, he said he knew he had the authority to do so and, therefore, asked for nobody's permission. He told me that two factors influenced his decision.

The first: "I knew there would be a big scramble to see who would head the series. I did not think such a scramble would be good for the series or Wake Forest. I knew I could do something to keep the scramble, bickering, and politics from happening."

The second: "I knew you had done an excellent job as George's assistant."

Gladding added that he "did not receive one complaint" about hiring me and "did have a number of people tell me what a good choice I had made."

So, what did I do to put myself in a position to become Trautwein's successor? Certainly, my close proximity to him at work enabled me to learn how he interacted with the artists' agents and managers, and the process of designing a season and selecting artists seemed less intimidating as time went on. But I can think of at least four other factors that helped me advance in the series' administration.

First, I always tried to execute my duties to Trautwein's satisfaction – even when, as will become evident later on this memoir, this meant going the extra mile after office hours.

Second, when it came time to pick Trautwein's successor, I could and did show I was capable of taking the series to the next level. I submitted a plan to Gladding that, among other things, called for a series website (which wasn't necessarily a given in 1998); pre-performance talks; and a committee of advisors charged with recommending performers for the series (more on that later). Neither Gladding nor I have been unable to unearth this plan, but he remembers it as "stellar," so it must have helped solidify his confidence in me.

Third, Trautwein, a professional conductor before he began working at Wake Forest, also taught academic courses at Wake Forest and conducted its orchestra. He spent a semester in India and a semester in Japan, having secured academic appointments in both instances. So, he was often absent from the series' offices for long periods of time. I used these moments not only to mind the store but also to demonstrate that I could think strategically like a manager:

During preparations for a series performance by Canadian Brass, for example, I persuaded Trautwein that the concert could be a golden opportunity to publicize and further a student-directed cause, the Brian Piccolo Cancer Fund Drive, which Wake Forest students created in 1980 to honor Piccolo, a former star running back at Wake Forest who died of cancer in 1970, when he was 26 years old. Piccolo also played several years professionally for a Chicago Bears team that featured Hall of Famers Gayle Sayers and Dick Butkus.

As fans of classic sports movies know, Piccolo's legacy was immortalized in the highly successful movie *Brian's Song*, which first aired on ABC in 1971. This film features a memorable theme called "The Hands of Time." At my suggestion, Canadian Brass played their arrangement of this music during their concert at Wake Forest. This was a very moving experience, since one of Piccolo's daughters, Tracey, then a student at Wake Forest, was recognized during the performance, and the series was able to devote a percentage of ticket revenue to the drive, along with donations of non-paying patrons. The Canadian Brass players signed their arrangement and gave it to me as a parting gift, which I considered among my most prized possessions until I gave it to the Secrest Artists Series archives in the Z. Smith Reynolds Library on the Wake Forest campus.

On another occasion, I showed I was management material when Ravi Shanker fell ill and had to cancel his series engagement at the last minute. Trautwein had obligations outside the office and the task of putting out this fire fell to me. I performed my duties deftly, getting the word out about the cancellation and answering related inquiries.

Fourth, each of my jobs before my series tenure had given me another way to stretch my competence and grow my confidence. Working with old people gave me patience, for example. I became more resourceful by working with military personnel, and I learned how to be flexible when I worked as a substitute teacher. I developed attributes that would benefit my work for the series, learning, for example, to think quickly, look beyond the immediate circumstance, and be positive. I believe that if one thinks positively and assumes the best of people, then almost anything can be accomplished. I've been accused of being too nice and too accommodating, but I really don't think those are flaws!

Part III

It Takes Grit, Smarts to Build an Audience

The Endless Challenge: Putting More Students in Seats

ONE OF MY PRIMARY OBJECTIVES as the series' director was to lure as many undergraduate students as possible to performances. This was no easy task, for several reasons.

For starters, I faced a good bit of competition from Wake Forest itself, thanks to all the other events on campus. These kept increasing during my tenure, jumping from a handful when it began to dozens by the time it ended. They included ACC basketball games, faculty lectures, Student Life and academic-department events as well as activities in residence halls and all the obligations of Greek life. The idea that a series event might be largely "protected" on the university's calendar was simply no longer a part of Wake

Forest life, as it had been during the early days of the Winston-Salem campus; at that time, it was policy to emphasize the arts in an academic setting, and conflicting calendaring was discouraged.

Moreover, many would-be student patrons arrived at Wake Forest with little or no experience with classical music, a core part of each series season, much less attending live performances of it. Their encounters with music often began and ended with what was on their electronic devices, and usually, it didn't include the masterworks of Beethoven or Brahms.

So, in many cases, a concert of classical music, even a free one in line with our mission of presenting the best established and emerging talent, did not top the list of free-time possibilities for students. The only students for whom the series was an easy sell were those from foreign countries, a growing segment of Wake Forest's student body, or those already involved in music, drama or dance at the university.What to do?

First off, I accepted the fact that attracting students to the series was going to be a struggle – but decided to keep a can-do mindset. I could have easily developed another attitude:

Early on in my tenure at Wake Forest, I attended a meeting of the North Carolina Presenters Consortium (ncpresenters.org). While there, I met the director of another university series, and he and I got to talking about how to attract more students to events. He had held his job for many years and was getting ready to retire.

"I gave up on students a long time ago," I recall him saying. "I'm just tired of trying to get them to go. I don't even market to them anymore. They get a discount, but they never come."

I resolved never to be sucked in by such negativity. I also learned to keep some perspective. If, for example, we attracted 200 student patrons to an orchestra concert in in the 2,250-seat Wait Chapel, I might be disappointed – but then hear that about 50 students attended a concert by the same orchestra at Duke University or UNC Chapel Hill, both of which have substantially more undergraduate students than Wake Forest. If I was disappointed about student turnout for a concert by a chamber ensemble, I remembered the time I went to Davidson College to hear a string quartet and noticed that just four of Davidson's students were in attendance.

I developed several strategies that I would continually use for attracting student patrons, and many had their origins in an important attribute I had begun developing in my earlier work life, as the recreation director of a women's prison. This was the ability to empathize with inmates in such a way that I might discover what motivated them to do more with their free time than watch television or hang out with other prisoners. "More" might mean some activity I had organized that would lead to a useful skill, such as knitting or sewing. Or it could mean arranging a theater troupe's performance of a play and workshop to stimulate empathy.

When I worked at Wake Forest, I was always trying to put myself in the shoes of the undergraduate students. I'd ask myself many questions: What's on the minds of these students? What are their ultimate aspirations? How can I get them to think about coming to the series? What prevents them from coming?

Increasingly, the answers reflected the fact that during my directorship, Wake Forest was changing from a reputable regional school with smart kids to a Top 25 school that served *really* smart ones, who were also ambitious, energetic, savvy and career-driven.

I concluded that Wake Forest's students needed to be shown how attending a series event would benefit them, both during and after their time at school. I came up with many ways to do that.

For example, if I could imagine certain students becoming wealthy doctors, lawyers or chief executives, I'd remind them that at some point, they'd be serving on the board of an arts organization.

"You don't want to be embarrassed," I'd say. "You want to know something about whatever art form you're asked to support. So, coming to Secrest events is in your best interest."

No two students' minds are exactly alike. Sometimes I'd get a blank look. And sometimes I'd be told I had a point.

Another strategy: In many instances, I found that I could entice students to patronize a series presentation if I offered them a meaningful encounter with performers before or after the performance.

Cellist Matt Haimovitz and pianist Christopher O'Riley were extremely helpful in this regard, as was the Student Union. In 2011, before Haimovitz and O'Riley presented "Shuffle. Play. Listen," Haimovitz did three "pop-up" performances with his cello around campus. O'Riley played the piano in the Student Center.

As for the Student Union, it screened films then, so during the fall of 1999 I arranged for two Charlie Chaplin films to be included in the union's lineup. These movies helped draw attention to a Secrest presentation in which Rick Benjamin led the Paragon Ragtime Orchestra in performances of music played during the screenings of three silent Chaplin classics.

I occasionally arranged for students to encounter a Secrest artist in a particular class or program at Wake Forest. Before their series performance, for example, cellist David Finckel and his wife, pianist Wu Han, offered a little Q-&-A session for students and faculty in the Office of Entrepreneurship at Wake Forest.

The two musicians had a lot to say about several of their entrepreneurial ventures, and they spoke of how they juggled their many duties, which included marriage, parenting, organizing, promoting, rehearsing and concertizing. They talked in detail about launching Music@Menlo, a San Francisco-area chamber music festival that features both performances and an institute for training the best emerging chamber musicians. And they illuminated what it took to get ArtistLed off the ground in 1997. ArtistLed, thought to be classical music's first musician-directed Internet-based recording company, has served as a model for similar independent labels.

A bottom-line truth was driven home, one that can be adapted to other fields. Even the best classical musicians must do more than play well, win competitions and count on management to discover them and line up concert dates; they also need to organize projects, promote themselves and do some hustling.

I didn't always have to reinvent the wheel when it came to ways of attracting student patrons. Some professors – and not just those who taught courses on the arts – would offer students extra credit if they went to a series event, continuing a practice that began before my directorship. Typically, extra credit at Wake Forest amounted to one of several things a student needed to do raise his or her grade.

I promoted the possibility of extra credit in the information I sent students. I always thanked professors who offered extra credit, as this amounted to a way of encouraging students to attend performances instead of requiring them. It seemed to me that if you required them, the students would come with a bad attitude.

Finally, I could play up the fact that the Secrest Artists Series does not charge Wake Forest students admission. This feature, which is rare among university presenters, removes a barrier to attendance for students, particularly those who are considering a range of extracurricular options.

Prospective Members of Fraternities, Sororities Attend Secrest Performances

About 45 percent of Wake's students belong to fraternities or sororities. That's a sizeable community on campus and in time I was able to enlist its help in getting more students to Secrest performances, though there were some rocky moments along the way.

During "rush" at Wake Forest, students must attend several events to become members of a particular fraternity or sorority. I worked with the school's appropriate administrator to make a Secrest performance one of those events. Typically, prospective Greeks would attend a single performance en masse.

In 2005, prospective Greeks were scheduled to be at a recital by Joshua Bell, a virtuoso violinist. There was just one problem: Wake Forest's men's basketball team was playing an ACC game against N.C. State that night as well, so I knew that getting large numbers of students to attend the performance would be next to impossible. I asked Bell's management if there was any wiggle room in the star violinist's schedule. Surprisingly, there was and the performance was moved to another night in the same week.

This was all really great news. What wasn't so great was that the prospective Greeks showed up late to the performance, which was held in Wait Chapel, sat in the back rows and proceeded to unleash a torrent of faux coughing as the music was played. (I found out later that this was called "the great Secrest cough-in.") The "coughing" became so bad that at one point, Bell stopped playing and said, "Gee, there's a lot of coughing going on."

Fortunately, I don't think Bell ever figured out exactly what was going on, and I wasn't about to tell him. At the end of the concert, he was given one of those tie-dyed shirts that Wake Forest fans wore at basketball games. He held it up and said, "Gee, Duke didn't give me one of these" – which was a real crowd-pleasing comment. (He had performed at Duke University just before his Wake Forest engagement.) He appeared to have left Winston-Salem with a warm memory.

I was furious at the behavior of the prospective Greeks and I made my anger known to the staff member overseeing them. He apologized and a similar incident never happened again. The culture of Greek life can be mysterious.

Perhaps, too, an important lesson was driven home: You can't expect that 19-year-old students will necessarily know correct etiquette for a concert of classical music. They need to be told, not only to be quiet but also to sit still and put away their cell phones and other electronic devices.

The Big Question: Was Our Attempt to Attract More Student Patrons Successful?

I would say yes. More often than not, as many as 500 students would attend the usually popular orchestra concerts in Wait Chapel, the larger of the two Secrest venues, and students would frequently fill about half the 560 seats in Brendle Recital Hall, which is better suited for chamber music, dance and small ensembles.

I acknowledge that free admission contributed to our success in attracting students to Secrest events, that it became a great way for me to sell the series. When Bell performed at Wake Forest, for example, I could tell potential student patrons that they would pay at least $70 to hear him play at another venue.

However, to call free admission a pivotal factor would be stretch. In 2016, when I wrote much of this memoir, presenters at Duke, UNC Chapel Hill and Davidson College were each charging students $10 for admission to their events. For most students at these schools, $10 amounts to chump change they'd often spend on pizza. It's an affordable price to pay for a presentation of first-rate music, drama or dance.

What was pivotal to our success in attracting students was never assuming that free admission *alone* would motivate students to come in droves to our concerts. The marketing strategies I developed – coupled with those my interns devised in their marketing plans (more on them later) – became a kind of insurance policy that would push students through our doors.

From time to time, there would be calls to charge Wake Forest's students admission to Secrest events, with some people arguing that a performance by top-rate professionals loses its value if it's free. I countered that free admission to our events both made them one of the special opportunities of a Wake Forest education and helped create community. Free admission for Wake Forest students (and for Wake's faculty and staff) remained policy during my directorship and continued to do so after my retirement. For that, I'm very grateful.

Part IV

Programming Reflects Advisors' Input, Various Connections

A New Way of Choosing Secrest Performers Emerges

BEGINNING IN 1985, I served as the series' secretary and, later, its coordinator, tending to various and sundry administrative and operations tasks. Trautwein, whom I succeeded as director, made all the programming decisions. He did not consult a committee when it came to choosing the artists who would perform each season.

When I became the director, in 1998, I put together a group of faculty members, administrators and students tasked with recommending the series' performers. I made this decision after much thought and for many reasons. For starters, my undergraduate degree was in fine arts, with an emphasis in theater. I had also done a good bit of ballet.

But my exposure to music, a key part of every series season, was limited to playing the piano and the harp. It did not make me the kind of an educated consumer of classical music who could determine, say, which of four outstanding string quartets to engage at Wake Forest.

From the beginning, I conceived of my advisors not as a formal, university-sanctioned committee but as a casual body called the Secrest Advisory Group. The people I picked for the group were to find it a fun experience. Some group members loved music, performed it at a high level and were very knowledgeable about the talent out there. They included Dr. Scott Klein, a professor of English and a fine pianist; the chair of the Department of Music (either Dr. Stewart Carter or Dr. David Levy); and Teresa Radomski, a Professor of Music in Voice. Two students, including the series intern, would always serve as Secrest advisors, as would several administrators, including Mary Gerardy, who held the title of Associate VP for Student Life.

The Secrest Advisory Group met two or three times a year. I'd present my advisors with a short list of people I really wanted for the series and ask them for their feedback. They would also contribute suggestions. Then, working from a spreadsheet with the artists' available dates, programs, fees and management, we'd all put together a series lineup that squared with the school calendar and the amount of money we had to spend. The aim was to finalize performance dates several months before a season began; the 2010-2011 season, for example, was decided by December of 2009.

We also made programming decisions that were in line with certain guiding principles. Chief among these was variety: We might like four great string quartets, for example, but not all of them could be included on a single series. We might favor Western classical music – but to me, it was also important to include artists from what I called an "ethnic" category, now more commonly called "world music."

We strove for programming that fulfilled the series' mission: to present the best of the established artists and the most promising of the emerging ones. These could be located on the Internet and every January in New York at the Association of Professional Arts Presenters' APAP|NYC, an annual conference at which presenters can book some of the best talent available because most of the leading talent agencies and managers are represented.

APAP|NYC showcases are held throughout Manhattan for the many new artists and/or programs by established ones. Though sometimes exhausting, the whole thing makes for an exciting and exhilarating four days. Despite the considerable expense, I attended APAP|NYC each year. That I always brought the series' intern along with me was a given: I considered it an investment in their education. We also enjoyed the added evening perk of attending Broadway shows or performances by the Metropolitan Opera.

Presenting the best of the established artists was sometimes a challenge. For example, I lobbied Joshua Bell's management for six years before he came to Wake Forest. The reason: The management of a "superstar" talent wants them to perform in the biggest halls of major cities, not in a smallish venue at a minor one.

Anyway, for the most part, the Secrest advisors and I ended up with people we liked, working together cordially. The only time that things got a little sensitive was when one of my advisors wanted a Native American artist. I did some serious research to find one but concluded that none of the possibilities were in keeping with our stature.

Connections, Connections

During my tenure as the series' director, I often forged connections that transformed a single Secrest event into a package that included the event and several related activities. This not only enhanced the educational impact of Secrest but also raised the profile of the series.

I found that connections could be particularly fruitful when I took advantage of Wake Forest University's considerable resources. A good example of this – and one mentioned earlier in this memoir – was the Q-&-A session that cellist David Finckel and his wife, pianist Wu Han, offered at the Office of Entrepreneurship at Wake Forest. I can point to several other examples where Wake Forest academic departments either provided a professor for a pre-performance talk or else helped advance the Secrest mission in other ways. The departments in question included Biology, English, Romance Languages, Religion, Theatre and Women's Studies. And, of course, the Department of Music co-sponsored numerous master classes led by virtuoso singers and instrumentalists who performed in the Secrest Artists Series and assisted in the payment of the extra fee. On occasion, these master classes were open to the public and to students from two nearby schools: Salem College and Winston-Salem State University.

In the Department of Biology at Wake Forest, Dr. Miles Silman, a prize-winning researcher, is the Andrew Sabin Family Foundation Professor of Conservation Biology and the Director of the Center for Energy, Environment, and Sustainability. He proposed that the Wayne Shorter Jazz Quartet be a Secrest presentation in the 2011-12 season and a fundraiser for the Amazon Aid Foundation. This idea took hold, and in time, several other related activities emerged to complement what we entitled "Jamazon." These included screenings of *Amazon Gold*, an award-winning documentary film by Sarah Dupont; a drumming workshop with the drummer in Wayne Shorter's quartet; and a Silman lecture on the Amazon rainforest crisis.

"Jamazon" wasn't the only example of Secrest's activism. Trumpeter Irvin Mayfield and the New Orleans Jazz Orchestra's Secrest performance took place in 2008, just a few years after Hurricane Katrina ravaged much of New Orleans. Mayfield also sat on the board of the New Orleans Public Library, and during his performance at Wake Forest, audience members could contribute to the library system, parts of which were severely damaged during the hurricane.

As for the Department of English, it offers students a minor in Medieval Studies. This was reflected in two English department-sponsored events I added to the 2011 Secrest presentation of Benjamin Bagby's *Beowulf*, described as "a modern take on the medieval English tradition of recitation with the accompaniment of a six-stringed harp." In the first, Bagby met with scholars from the medieval literature program for a Q-&-A session. The second, very successful event was a post-performance reception at which mead, cheeses and dark breads were served to scores of *Beowulf* enthusiasts.

In 2006, as part of a Secrest presentation titled "Radio Kaboul: Ustad Mahwash & Friends," Women's Studies invited Mahwash to a luncheon for its students and faculty. Mahwash is the greatest female singer in Afghanistan and she is the only female allowed to sing on the radio there. She made quite an impression on the students and professors at the luncheon, even though she needed to be discreet when it came to commenting about her country's politics.

One last case illustrates how helpful Wake Forest's resources could be to the series. Several days before L.A. Theatre Works presented "Top Secret: Battle for the Pentagon Papers" in Wait Chapel, Daniel Ellsberg – a Department of Defense employee who released those papers to the press – spoke in "Voices of Our Time," the premier lecture series on campus. The papers, a top-secret government history of the Vietnam War, revealed that the U.S. government had deceived the American public about America's involvement in the war.

A decision by *The New York Times* to publish the papers unleashed a battle pitting proponents of a free press against Nixon administration officials who wanted to keep the papers secret. After attending Ellsberg's lecture, Secrest patrons could later in the week watch L.A. Theatre Works' radio drama re-enactment of this battle play out in a semi-staged performance in Wait Chapel.

Collaborate, Collaborate

During my directorship, it became increasingly common for multiple arts organizations of Winston-Salem to join forces for projects that might be too expensive or challenging for one arts group to take on alone. I made the Secrest Artists Series a part of this trend, arranging collaborative efforts with such organizations as the Arts Council of Winston-Salem and Forsyth County, Authoring

Action, the Winston-Salem Symphony and Reynolda House Museum of American Art.

In the fall of 2002, ArtsIgnite, a multidisciplinary arts festival organized by the local arts council, ignited all over Winston-Salem. At the request of late Phil Hanes, an arts philanthropist extraordinaire who served as a principal organizer of the festival, Secrest programmed a "signature event" for the festival that would appeal to the entire community. At first, star mezzo-soprano Frederica von Stade was booked, which seemed to please everyone, but she later cancelled for health reasons.

In short time, tenor Ben Heppner emerged as a suitable replacement and I was able to book him for a fee lower than von Stade's. He also led a master class for students from Wake Forest's Department of Music, and he attended a lovely reception at Reynolda House that followed the performance.

Reynolda House, incidentally, is among the leading tourist attractions in Winston-Salem. In 2004, Leonard Slatkin, then the music director of the National Symphony Orchestra (NSO), visited the museum's treasures and was the honored guest during a Q-&-A luncheon at Reynolda House before the NSO's concert in Wait Chapel.

In 2005, the NSO chose North Carolina as the site of its American Residency for that year, having accepted an invitation from the North Carolina Arts Council. (Between 1992 and 2011, the American Residency program brought the NSO to a different state each year; a residency would include several NSO concerts along with NSO musicians participating in dozens of outreach and educational activities.) An NSO staffer told me that the orchestra's positive experiences in Winston-Salem were pivotal in its decision to establish a residency in North Carolina.

As for the Winston-Salem Symphony, two notable collaborations with that organization come to mind. In 2001, when Denyce Graves, a star mezzo-soprano, sang with the symphony, they presented three performances: one in Wait Chapel at Wake Forest (as part of the series) and two in the Stevens Center, the downtown venue where the symphony usually performs its "Classics" programs. The symphony and the series entered into a partnership where the symphony paid its musicians to perform in all three concerts, while Secrest provided funding for Graves' fee.

Ticket revenue from the concert in Wait Chapel went to Secrest, and ticket revenue from the Stevens Center performances went to the symphony. A similar Secrest-symphony partnership underpinned percussionist Evelyn Glennie's 2008 appearance with the symphony.

Secrest Reaches Out to Students in Winston-Salem's Public Schools

From time to time during my directorship, various Secrest performers either introduced their art to the students of

Winston-Salem's public schools or led master classes for them.

The Salzburg Marionette Theater, which I programmed for Secrest in 2001, proved particularly adept at appealing not only to adults but also to young children age 9 or 10. The group specializes in staging performances of opera that use 2-foot marionettes on a tiny stage; recordings accompany the puppets.

The Salzburg puppeteers presented their version of Mozart's *The Magic Flute* three times in Wake Forest's MainStage Theatre (which in 2016, was renamed the Harold C. Tedford Stage in honor of Tedford, a Professor Emeritus of Theatre). In addition, as part of a field trip to Wake Forest's campus, 4^{4t} graders from Bolton Elementary watched a special performance by the Salzburg Marionette Theater, talked to the puppeteers, and learned about the history of puppetry.

The Salzburg Marionette Theater also visited Brenner Children's Hospital, where they entered some hospital rooms and presented short non-staged performances for small numbers of patients. The puppeteers commented that they had never done anything similar in Europe and found the experience very moving.

Reynolds High School, also called the Richard J. Reynolds Magnet School for the Visual and Performing Arts, is home to the Judy Voss Jones Arts Center and the R.J. Reynolds Memorial Auditorium, a majestic theater used not only by students but also by professional performers. It is a hotbed of artistic activity for teenagers and those who teach them.

So, it made sense for the series to do some outreach at Reynolds High. In 2009, this happened in a big way when the series presented "Danzón: Luna Negra Dance Theater with the Turtle Island String Quartet and Paquito D'Rivera" in Reynolds Auditorium.

The performance, the first Secrest Artists Series event to be presented off Wake Forest's campus, resulted from a collaboration of Reynolds High's Arts Magnet program and Wake Forest's Department of Romance Languages.

In a sense, Romance Languages paved the way for "Danzón," having produced "Cuban Artists' Books and Prints: 1985-2008," an exhibit on view until a week before the "Danzón" October performance. Before its official evening presentation for the series' usual patrons, the "Danzón" performers not only offered a special presentation of their show for all of Reynolds' students; they also led workshops for the school's string players and for high school and college dancers. Reynolds High and Secrest shared the cost of these activities.

In short, Reynolds High students benefited from rubbing elbows with the performers of "Danzón." Unfortunately, the same cannot be said of Authoring Action's interactions with some performers of "Abraham Inc.," which Secrest presented in 2011.

The "Abraham" performers included clarinetist David Krakauer, trombonist Fred Wesley and the hip-hop artist Socalled. Authoring Action – whose founding co-directors include the Rev. Lynn Rhoades and Nathan Ross Freeman – is dedicated to developing teenagers into "authors and articulate advocates for social change."

I arranged for Krakauer and a few other "Abraham" musicians to watch theatrical presentations of Authoring Action members delivering their texts out loud. It proved to be a weak event, because the teens were too selfish and immature to realize the value of the experience.

Part V

The Best Help Is Sometimes Free

I TOOK SEVERAL STEPS TO ENHANCE the educational value of the Secrest Artists Series. One of the most important was engaging a WFU student to serve as an unpaid intern each year. My goal was twofold – purely selfish because I needed help, and altruistic in the desire to produce hands-on learning for an interested student.

The interns helped me with various administrative and day-of-performance tasks, and they learned much about what goes on behind the scenes of a performing-arts presenter. I expected interns to put in at least 10 hours a week for me, and, after getting them excused from classes and other commitments, required them to be by my side on the day of a performance and for most of the day that preceded it.

I keep in touch with many of my former interns. Several of them – including Hayden Barnes, who was the Winston-Salem Symphony's marketing director for several years and became the manager of Secrest Artists Series after I retired – either pursued careers in arts administration after graduating or volunteered for arts organizations in their hometowns. No matter what they do, they're the kind of strong, productive citizens our increasingly tough world needs.

Of course, just because you establish an internship doesn't mean that students will necessarily clamor to fill it, especially when there isn't any remuneration. Fortunately, at least two factors helped my recruitment efforts. First, several interns – including Anne Hillgartner, a music performance major who played clarinet in WFU ensembles, and Mariama Holman, the founding president of the Black and Gold Jazz Club at Wake Forest – were already participating in the arts at Wake Forest before they began working with me. They viewed a series internship as a great way to take their arts experiences at Wake Forest to another level. An internship "really made you feel ownership of an important part of campus life," Hillgartner told me recently. "That became my motivation."

Second, as mentioned earlier in this memoir, I could offer prospective interns quite a carrot – participation in the Association of Professional Arts Presenters' APAP | NYC.

By the time my directorship ended, as many as six students were vying to fill an intern position. I tended to give preference to winners of the renewable Presidential Scholarships of $16,000 each that go annually to students with exceptional talent in art, dance, debate, music and theatre. The Presidential Scholars are expected to participate actively in their areas of talent.

I looked for self-starters with good people and time-management skills who could a) recognize a need and do something about it or b) come up with good ideas and follow through on them. Jared Lilly, who served as my intern during the 2007-2008 school year, completed NYU's graduate program in performing arts administration in 2016. He typified the qualities I wanted in an intern. "He followed through on assignments, initiated new projects, and supervised volunteers with grace and charm," I wrote on his LinkedIn page. "His curiosity, diligence, and creativity served him well and contributed to the success of the program."

The Secrest Artists Series had but one paid staff member – me. So, interns were invaluable, often taking on crucial responsibilities that I just couldn't manage. Among other things, each intern developed and executed their own yearly marketing plan aimed at students; helped generate publicity for the series in Wake Forest's newspaper; managed the box office and volunteer ushers on performance nights; and supervised work-study students, who did things such as putting up series posters around campus and taking them down. I usually assigned interns tasks that complemented their strengths; these ranged from writing grant proposals, one of intern Lauren Stephenson's strengths, to planning a menu for a post-concert reception, which Lilly did superbly well.

My interns had lots of great ideas, particularly when it came to marketing the series to students. Thus, my job was not to throw up roadblocks but to encourage action. As Holman said recently, I gave her free rein to do just about anything to market the series – as long as it could be financed, the right resources were behind the effort, nobody would be offended and, ultimately, it would add value to what we were doing. Hillgartner echoed these sentiments: "For the first time, somebody took me seriously and led me along."

When it came to creative marketing, both Holman and Hillgartner put in stellar efforts. Holman worked to break down barriers between the artist and the consumer, who's often a member of a fraternity or a sorority at Wake Forest. When it came to a 2011 performance of Benjamin Bagby's *Beowulf*, she did that by organizing a party with the *Beowulf* theme.

As for Hillgartner, she came up with a neat way to attract attention to Shorter's 2012 concert. Inspired by the Amazon Aid Foundation raising awareness of environmental issues in the Amazon rain forest, she had different-colored plastic frogs affixed to cards and placed them all over campus. By each frog were words on the card that read: "Save Me. Flip Over to Find Out How."

Part VI

Persevering

ONE OF MY CHIEF RESPONSIBILITIES was keeping artists happy – even when, as sometimes happened, their demands became unexpected challenges I had to meet at the 11th hour.

Exhibit A: Ruth Laredo (and Charlie Rose)

In the early 1990s, while serving as Trautwein's assistant, I oversaw the care and maintenance of artists before, during and after their performances.

Pianist Ruth Laredo was among the series' performers in 1993. One fall day, I picked her up at the Piedmont Triad International Airport in Greensboro and drove her to her accommodations, the Wake Forest University-owned Graylyn Estate on Reynolda Road. Graylyn was originally the home of Bowman Gray Sr. (1874-1935), the former

Chairman of the Board of R.J. Reynolds Tobacco Co., and his wife, Nathalie Lyons Gray (1884-1961). In 1993, it had not yet been refitted as the Graylyn Conference Center. It was more like a private boutique hotel.

Anyway, all seemed to be going well with Laredo until I received a call at my home from her about 10pm. Her room in Graylyn did not have a television, she told me. (At that time, none of Graylyn's rooms had television because the establishment was a place of peace and tranquility and reflected the period in which it was built). Laredo said she could not sleep unless she watched *Charlie Rose* every night on PBS; if Graylyn did not have a television she needed to move into new quarters.

Well, all this happened during the High Point Market, which bills itself as the world's largest furnishings industry trade show, so hotel rooms were at a premium throughout the Piedmont Triad. Fortunately, I had a contact at the Adams Mark Hotel (now the Winston-Salem Marriott) in downtown Winston-Salem and he produced a suitable room. I drove to Graylyn (which is about a 25-minute drive), picked up Laredo and took her to the Adams Mark. She got her *Charlie Rose* fix, slept well and, most important, gave a good performance.

Exhibit B: Denyce Graves and Her Former Husband

The performance by Denyce Graves was one of the most memorable in all my time with the Secrest Artists

Series. It was also one of the most enervating, thanks to a crowded schedule of events surrounding her performance and to some backstage drama at one of three performances she sang with the Winston-Salem Symphony.

In February 2001, when Graves performed in Winston-Salem, her stardom had been rising fast, thanks to some great recordings and several well-received *Carmen* performances at the Metropolitan Opera.

Her schedule in Winston-Salem befitted that stardom. It included a rehearsal with the Winston-Salem Symphony, a luncheon at Winston-Salem State University, a master class with WFU and Winston Salem State University students, and a reception given by the now-defunct Wachovia Bank in the lobby of their new building in downtown Winston-Salem. Graves teamed up with the symphony to present three performances: one on campus in Wait Chapel (for the series), and two in the Stevens Center, the symphony's principal venue. I was responsible for getting her to all the performances and events and for making sure all her needs were met in the process.

Backstage arrangements for the artists performing in Wait Chapel are very awkward. There is only one ladies room, and I had to label it specifically for Graves. Despite the "Ms. Graves" sign on the door, during intermission one of the audience members darted in the room!

Well, Graves' former husband, the guitarist David Perry, witnessed the mishap and became distraught. He demanded a can of cleaning spray or disinfectant to clean his wife's bathroom. In a stroke of luck, I spied a custodial cleaning cart at the end of the hall, retrieved a can of Lysol, and gave it to Perry. He then treated the restroom. To this day, I'm not certain if he ever told Graves what happened. The couple divorced shortly after Graves' performance in Winston-Salem.

The entire Graves visit, which lasted several days, was almost too much for one staffer (me) to manage and by the end of it I was exhausted. As I was driving home on a Sunday afternoon, after Graves' last performance with the symphony, a policeman stopped me for a minor traffic violation and I collapsed into tears. He took pity and let me go.

And just before I arrived home, I stopped at a Harris Teeter grocery store to buy a small item. The cashier asked me where I had been so "all dressed up" and I told her. "Oh wow, I wanted to go to that but I had to work," she said. And I wept again. A cashier at Harris Teeter knew about Denyce Graves and Secrest. Wow!

Exhibit C:

Ben Heppner and the Case of the Missing Program Bio

As mentioned earlier, the Secrest performance of Ben Heppner was one of those included in the ArtsIgnite Festival. All went well with preparations and arrangements – until the night of the performance:

I had booked Heppner and Craig Rutenberg, his accompanist, into Graylyn. I picked them up there and drove them to the performance, providing each with concert programs.

As I drove, Rutenberg, who was sitting in the backseat, looked over the program. He quietly asked: "Lillian, why isn't my bio included in the program?"

Oh, dear. Although CAMI, Rutenberg's management, had not sent me any information on him, I had also neglected to ask for it.

Well, by the time we discovered that Rutenberg's bio was missing, it was 6:30 pm and the performance was scheduled to begin an hour later. I tried not to panic. Matthew Webb, my intern at the time, was much more computer-savvy than I was. I explained the importance and urgency of the situation and asked him to find a bio online, then download and make hundreds of copies of it. He did and we had enough copies for the student ushers to stuff into the programs, at the last minute. Rutenberg was pleased and grateful.

Part VII

The Piano

WHO KNEW THE CRITICAL ROLE of the piano in a concert series? Well, of course I knew that a good piano was important, but the time, energy and expense in the care of a Steinway Concert Grand D was an education in itself! Wake Forest had been given a fine concert instrument in the 1950s by some generous local donors. A plaque above the keyboard noted that it was first played in 1968 by Artur Rubenstein. It belonged exclusively to no particular office or department, was kept, locked, on the platform in Wait Chapel and used by those with access to the key. (Wake Forest Baptist Church, the Department of Music, the Artists Series, occasionally rented the piano for a community event and it was used at large university events that required a piano). Over time, it became abused and misused and in bad shape. The decision was made by Trautwein to move the piano to Brendle Hall and assign the maintenance responsibility to the Artists Series. That took care of the abuse problem, except that the side stage doors were a tight squeeze in rolling the piano on and off the stage and the edges of the case began to look rather beaten. A special grant from the Provost's office funded the refurbishment of the instrument, which included replacement of critical parts and the regulation and voicing, as well as the refinishing of the case.

Fortunately, Wake Forest employed John Chapman, a certified Steinway technician, on a contract basis to tune and care for all the pianos on campus. The Steinway D was very important to him and he became indispensable when we presented a noted pianist. World-class artists deserve world-class instruments and, for the most part, the pianists we presented were content with our Steinway.

Chapman would be on hand when the artist arrived in the hall and make any adjustments that were requested. Most of these required another tuning during intermission and Chapman was always accommodating. Written in Sharpie under the lid and on the brass plate are the signatures of all the pianists who performed for Secrest. Chapman suggested that we ask the artists to do so, along with their date of performance, and I thought it was a terrific idea. Among the signatures are those for Philippe Entremont, Orion Weiss, Menachem Presslar, Wu Han, Steven Hough, Angela

Hewitt, Arcadi Volodos, Alicia de Larrocha, Ruth Laredo, Marc-Andre Hamelin, and Christopher O'Reilly.

Acoustics in Brendle Hall are very fine and artists were always very appreciative. Moving the piano for an event in Wait Chapel was always an expensive undertaking. In Dr. Charles Allen's early days as director of the Artists Series, he would recruit students on the spot to move the piano on and off the platform in Wait Chapel. But in later years, for a number of obvious reasons, it became necessary to hire a professional piano mover to move the Steinway 150 yards from the Brendle stage to Wait Chapel, a $400 round-trip expense.

In about 2008, the Department of Music purchased its own Steinway D. Unselfishly, they allowed Secrest the luxury of offering our artists a choice of pianos for their performance. John would prepare both instruments, and it was so interesting to watch their selection process.

Part VIII

Secrest Becomes Known for Its Arresting Posters

WHEN I RETIRED FROM THE SERIES, in 2013, I received the perfect gift to mark the occasion: a collage of posters, each of which Hayes Henderson had designed for a different series season beginning in the early 1990s.

Since 2010, Henderson, an award-winning designer, has been the Assistant Vice President of Creative Communications at Wake Forest. Previously, he worked at one of two studios he started.

Working with Henderson was one of the most rewarding parts of my job. We would meet once a year to discuss everything from the artists I had engaged for a coming season to my observations about how the last season had gone. We also traded notes about how our children were doing – during our partnership; they went from grade school to marriage.

After Henderson and I talked, he'd go back to his studio and start thinking. In time, he'd return with a range of sketches and we'd discuss the merits of each before arriving at a consensus about which one likely worked best.

Henderson's Secrest posters are marked by what he describes as "a rawness and spontaneity." They feature hand-drawn elements that are scanned and manipulated. They reflect the fact that "consideration of how the type interplayed with image was nearly as important as the conceptualization of the image itself," Henderson said in an interview for this memoir.

Henderson also said that he lacks the "whiz-bang chops" that some folks have in Photoshop.

"I actually saw that as a strength rather than limitation, something to keep me focused on the overall rather than the effect," he said. "I feel so many people learn all the chords but don't really know how to write a tune. I'm like the guy that can play three chords (but) knows how to twist them a lot of ways."

Henderson's Secrest posters were important for at least two reasons. First, they became sought-after collector items, adorning Winston-Salem homes and the offices of Wake Forest University professors. Henderson sometimes delivered posters past the agreed delivery date and when that happened, faculty would call and ask when to expect the posters.

Second, Henderson's posters won a number of important design awards and were often noted in trade publications read by designers. As such they got the kind of attention that enabled him to recruit some very talented designers into his studio.

"And that's back when there weren't a ton of good designers in the area," Henderson recalled. "I was able to get folks here who may not have come to Winston-Salem if we were not doing work that was showing up in publications. So, in no small way, Secrest was a big part of that."

Epilogue

ABOUT FIVE YEARS HAVE PASSED since I left Wake Forest University to live in Florida with my husband, Tom, who retired as senior pastor of Winston-Salem's Friedberg Moravian Church. In this new chapter of my life, I have engaged in some serious thinking about my working life – and, by far, the position of longest duration and greatest joy was as the Director of the Secrest Artists Series.

Yes, I had had some memorable experiences before I began working for the series. For example, as Program Director at the Armed Services YMCA in Newport, Rhode Island, I experienced what seemed like a USO operation in World War II. As a recreation director at a women's prison in Rhode Island, I glimpsed the life of women caught in the consequences of poor decisions (mostly provoked by abuse, poverty, poor education, and family environment). And at a senior center in small-town Pennsylvania, I grew to appreciate the perspectives of an older generation.

But at Wake Forest, I flourished in an environment of higher learning, high expectation, and high culture. It was fascinating to engage with professors at the top of their fields and with students exploring their potential fields of interest. That I was promoted from the series' Coordinator, a largely administrative-support position, to its Director was a particularly gratifying accomplishment.

Introducing students to classical music in all its iterations was a challenge worth meeting. I wanted the students to understand that experiencing the best of the classics and the most promising of new performance work was a rich part of their education.

I'm still astonished that in the 1920s, Wake Forest decided to include a performing arts series in the extracurricular life of its students – and to make it free of charge for everyone in the University community: students, staff, and faculty. But that is exactly what the administration at Wake Forest College, on the old campus near Raleigh, decided to do. The series occasionally included speakers and was not presented on a consistent basis.

When Wake Forest moved to Winston-Salem, in 1956, the series continued with an even larger profile and purpose. It continued to be run by a professor with student volunteer help until 1985, when I became the paid assistant to Trautwein.

Prior to Trautwein, the series had only three directors: Dr. Charles Allen (for a very long time), who was a Professor of Biology and astute lover of classical music; Bill Ray; and Dr. David Levy, a professor of music.

Each one of my predecessors brought well-developed taste, sensibility and considerable intelligence to selecting artists they wanted to bring to Wake Forest. They kept the standards high. In many ways their struggles were the same as I encountered – the biggest one being attracting student patrons, for whom the series was designed. Alas, some things never do change!

Still, one of the many ways that Wake Forest has distinguished itself is offering its students the (free) opportunity to take in performances by the very best of the established artists and the most promising of the new. That's quite a legacy and I worked hard to uphold it during my directorship of the series.

Allen wrote a very detailed history of his tenure with the series – which was a big help to me – detailing his challenges with readying Wait Chapel for performances (Brendle Hall was not yet built), attracting a student audience, finding technical assistance, and dealing with artists' eccentricities.

Allen's history also reveals that at one point, the series had very large group of subscribers from the general, non-university public of Winston-Salem. They were drawn to the series because there was no Stevens Center (until 1983);

no UNC School of the Arts (which began operating in 1965); and few other regional presenters of performing artists with international reputations.

A copy of Allen's history is in the Archives of Wake Forest University and in the possession of Dr. Scott Klein, the current director. I'm honored to contribute to the historical record that Allen helped compile. Although I have considered using my interest and skill in the arts management field as a faculty adjunct, consultant, or advisor, I am content to consider this chapter closed. There are other interests to explore, such as horticulture (I am now certified as a Master Gardener by the University of Florida), writing, and studio art. I can also simply bask in my beautiful home surroundings.

Earlier on in this memoir, I mentioned that my father worked for General Electric for a time after he retired from the Air Force. After his contract with GE expired, he bought property in rural Volusia County, Florida, where he built a lovely home and focused on raising cows and horses. This is where I now live – a beautiful, peaceful pastoral setting with live oaks and azaleas – and our two children and eight grandchildren visit us often.

As I look back on my tenure at Wake Forest, another true highlight emerges in my memory. This was enrolling, in 2003, as a graduate student in the Master of Arts in Liberal Studies (MALS) program. In 2006, after finishing intensive course work and writing my thesis, I earned my master's degree. Like this memoir, my thesis will contribute to the written history of Wake Forest; it's cast as a "biography" of the house that is now the home of the Wake Forest president. (The house was given to the university by local arts philanthropist Dewitt Chatham Hanes, and it has a fascinating history.)

I'm grateful I pursued a master's degree at Wake Forest because it introduced me in hands-on fashion to a very high caliber of teaching, the challenging life of the mind of a student and, of course, the expansion of knowledge. I loved every moment of being a student.

I hold Wake Forest tightly in my heart and memories, especially Ed ("Mr. Wake Forest") Wilson, Provost Emeritus; Gladding; the late Ed Christman, who served as Chaplain for 30 years before retiring in 2003; and Harold Tedford, Professor Emeritus of Theatre. They were and are legends and giants in the guiding of the university.

Many of my former student interns are in touch with me. One, Hayden Barnes, is now the manager of the Secrest Artists Series. What a fitting close to a happily satisfying experience.

Lillian Shelton
November 2018

AUTHOR BIOS

Lillian Britt Shelton began working in the administration of the Secrest Artists Series in 1985, serving as its Director from 1998 until 2013, the year she retired. Along the way, she earned a Master of Arts in Liberal Studies from Wake Forest. With a B.A. degree in Fine Arts (emphasis in Theatre) from St. Andrews College in Laurinburg, NC, she headed for the bright lights and big city of New York in the late 1960s. After a theatre career that never really started, she enjoyed employment with the National Council of Churches in NYC, the Armed Services YMCA in Newport, RI, the Rhode Island Correctional Institute for Women and the Area Agency for Aging in Bethlehem, Pa. – proving that a liberal arts degree prepares one for almost anything!

Ken Keuffel, a former arts reporter at the *Winston-Salem Journal*, lives in Winston-Salem. His many freelance assignments include ghostwriting the memoirs of artists, other creatives and anyone who works in support of them; see www.recordingyourstory.com for more details.

Made in the USA
Columbia, SC
18 November 2020

24871694R00043